AF891532

Exam FA2

Maintaining Financial Records

Pocket Notes

KAPLAN PUBLISHING

British library cataloguing-in-publication data

A catalogue record for this book is available from the British Library.

Published by:
Kaplan Publishing UK
179-191 Borough High Street
London
SE1 1HR

ISBN 978-1-83735-289-0

Printed and bound in Great Britain.

Contents

Preface

These Pocket Notes contain everything you need to know for the exam, presented in a unique visual way that makes revision easy and effective.

Written by experienced lecturers and authors, these Pocket Notes break down content into manageable chunks to maximise your concentration.

Quality and accuracy are of the utmost importance to us so if you spot an error in any of our products, please send an email to mykaplanreporting@kaplan.com with full details, or follow the link to the feedback form in MyKaplan.

Our Quality Co-ordinator will work with our technical team to verify the error and take action to ensure it is corrected in future editions.

This document references IFRS® Accounting Standards and IAS® Accounting Standards, which are authored by the International Accounting Standards Board (the Board), and issued prior to 31 August 2025.

Introduction

In this chapter

- Overview of the examination.
- Key syllabus areas.

Overview of the examination

This examination will consist of:

50 compulsory objective test questions for two marks each	100
Total marks	100

The examination duration is two hours. The pass mark is 50%.

The examination is available as a computer-based examination.

As the examination consists entirely of objective test questions, you do need to consider the following:

- Objective test questions allow the examiner to cover a significant amount of the syllabus within each examination. This means you cannot simply learn only part of the syllabus and hope to achieve a pass standard – you will need to learn the entire syllabus to maximise your chances of success in the examination.
- As part of your revision, work through the questions in the study text and any question banks you may have to ensure you understand the style of question asked.
- You should ensure that you allocate your time correctly so that you can answer all questions.
- Remember in the examination, you can answer questions in any order (as long as you complete the objective test correctly). It is therefore worth completing the easier questions first and then re-visiting the more difficult questions before the end of the examination. This approach will (hopefully) ensure you have obtained the easy marks first and avoid missing them should you run out of time.

Finally, when all else fails, guess – there is no negative marking.

Objective test question styles

- Multiple choice – where you are required to choose one answer from a list of options provided by clicking on the appropriate 'radio button'
- Multiple response – where you are required to select more than one response from the options provided by clicking on the appropriate tick boxes (typically choose two options from the available list)
- Multiple response matching – where you are required to indicate a response to a number of related statements by clicking on the 'radio button' which corresponds to the appropriate response for each statement
- Number entry – where you are required to key in a response to a question shown on the screen

Key syllabus areas

The aim of FA2 is to develop knowledge and understanding of the underlying principles and concepts relating to Maintaining Financial Records and technical proficiency in the use of double-entry accounting techniques including the preparation of basic financial statements.

On completion of FA2 candidates should be able to:

- Explain generally accepted accounting principles and concepts.
- Outline the principles and process of basic bookkeeping.
- Prepare journals and ledger accounts.
- Record transactions and events.
- Prepare a trial balance (including identifying and correcting errors).
- Reconciliations
- Prepare financial statements
- Partnerships

chapter

1

Accounting principles, concepts and charateristics

In this chapter

- The basic principles of financial reporting.
- Characteristics of useful financial information.
- Accounting policies.
- The users of financial information.
- Accounting records and documents.
- The regulatory framework.

The basic principles of financial reporting

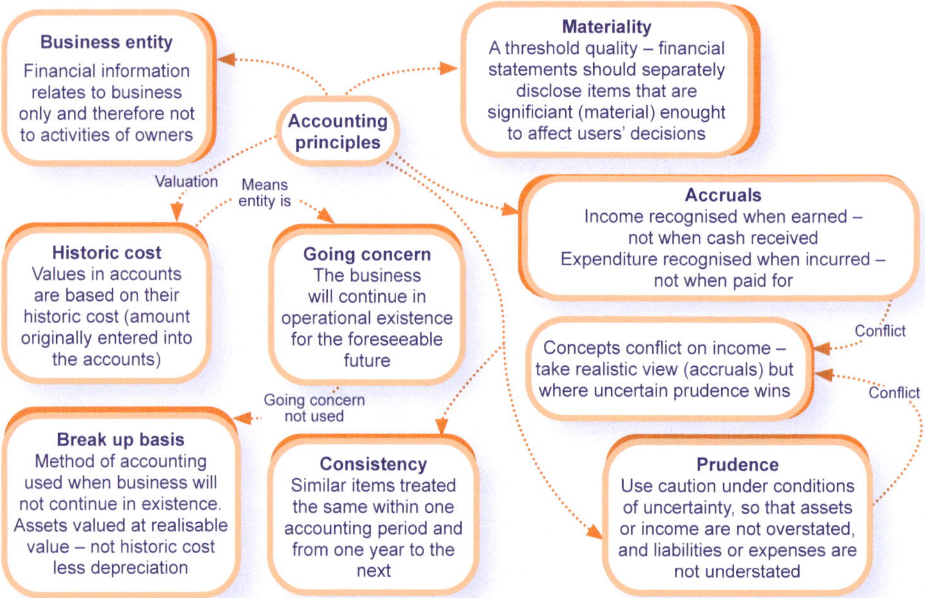

Characteristics of useful financial information

Two fundamental qualitative characteristics	
Relevance	Information is relevant if it capable of making a difference in the decisions made by users. This is likely to be the case when information can be used to confirm current understanding and/or to or predict future outcomes. Materiality is one aspect of relevance - information is material if its omission or misstatement could influence the decisions of users of the financial statements.
Faithful representation	Information should be faithfully represented. This means that accounting information should be presented in accordance with best practice and that the commercial substance of transactions should be presented in the financial statements, rather than their strict legal form. This would imply that such information is complete, neutral or free from bias and free from material error.
Four enhancing qualitative characteristics	
Comparability	Users must be able to compare the financial statements of an enterprise over time to identify trends in its financial position and performance. Users must also be able to compare the financial statements of **different enterprises** to evaluate their relative financial positions, performance and financial adaptability.
Verifiability	Information should be capable of either direct verification or indirect verification.
Timeliness	This means that users of information have access to that information within timescales which are appropriate for their decision-making purposes.
Understandability	Information in financial statements must be understandable to its users. This may depend upon how knowledgeable individuals are when evaluating financial information.

Accounting policies

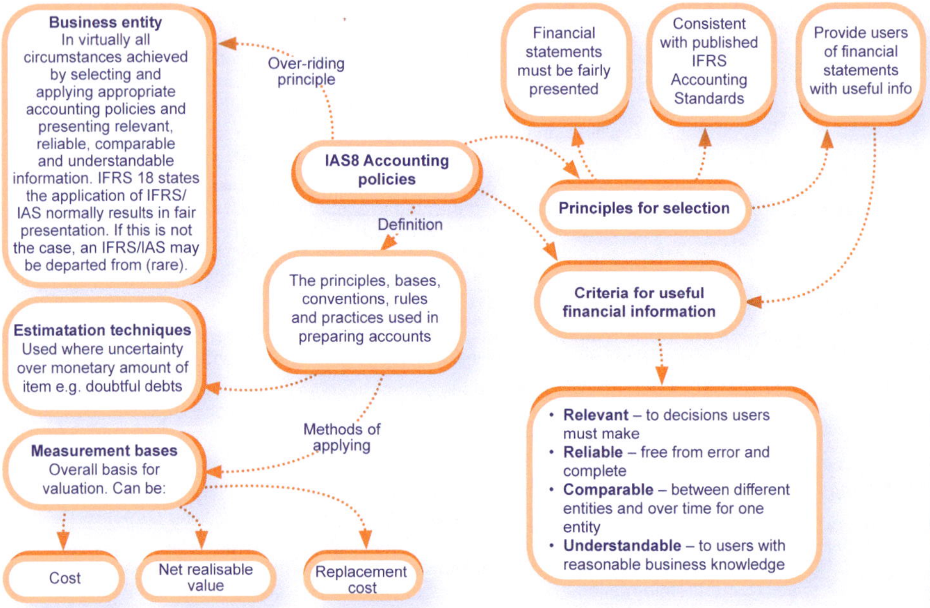

The users of financial information

User	Information needed
Owner	Determine drawings. Improve business performance
Investors	Whether to invest/withdraw capital from the business
Lenders	Check whether loans can be repaid
Suppliers	Ensure entity will pay for goods supplied
Employees	Check company will continue to pay wages
Customers	Ensure business will continue to exist (essential when the business is being relied on e.g. support contracts)
Government	Check tax paid is correct
Public	Monitor business activities (e.g. pressure groups)

Exam focus

If a question asks you to identify why users need financial information, suggest reasons specific to certain users rather than generic to all.

Accounting records and documents

Documents – essential contents

Sales invoices/Purchase invoices

- Customer name and address
- Name of business, business address and telephone number
- Invoice number
- Invoice date
- Customer account reference
- Order number
- Goods: quantity, description, price
- Total invoice value
- Settlement terms

Purchase orders

- Business name of buyer
- Registered office and company registration number
- Supplier name and address
- Purchase order number
- Business contact
- Delivery date

Key Point

- Sales invoice sent from company to customer for goods supplied.
- Purchase invoice received from a company for goods purchased.

Key documents in credit sales/purchases systems

Sales system

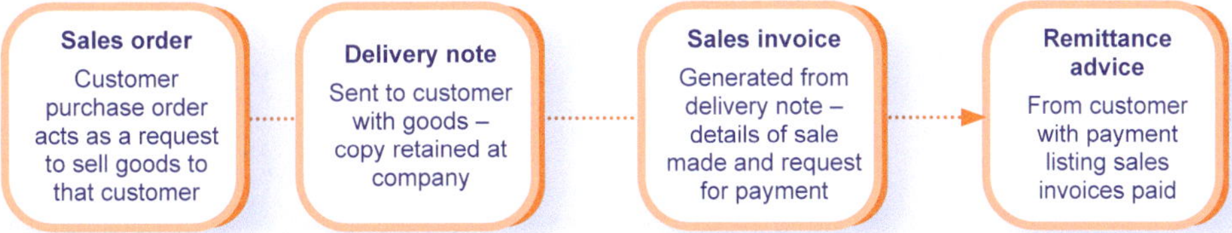

Purchase system

Other business documents

Statement of account
Sent monthly to customer showing invoices not yet paid

Credit note
Sent from supplier to customer, cancels part or whole of invoice for goods returned

Debit note
A document raised by a customer and issued to a supplier to request a credit note.

Petty cash voucher
Shows authorised expenditure from petty cash supported by documentation showing expense is genuine

Employee payslip
Notification to employee of wages earned less statutory and other authorised deductions

Contents of the payslip:

- employee's / employer's name
- date
- total gross pay split into elements e.g overtime, etc
- any employee pension contribution
- deductions from, or adjustments to, pay
- total gross pay to date
- total tax paid to date in tax year and tax due this pay day
- National Insurance/social security contributions due this pay day
- net pay.

Exam focus

Remember many of the multiple-choice questions on this section are factual so ensure you remember the names of the different types of business documents and what each is used for.

The regulatory framework

International Financial Reporting standards/International Accounting Standards (collectively referred to as IAS Accounting Standards) are a set of rules and guidelines, issued by a body formed within the accountancy profession, governing the preparation and presentation of the annual financial statements of limited companies that purport to show a 'true and fair view'.

There may also be national laws or regulations to comply with, such as those for document retention.

Sole traders and partnerships do not normally have to comply with IAS Accounting Standards. However, sole traders and partnerships tend to apply the principles of the standards as they represent best accounting practice. The tax authorities and other external users often take the view that financial statements should be prepared in accordance with applicable financial reporting standards.

Exam focus

Questions dealing with the definitions, particularly relating to the qualitative characteristics of useful financial information and the different business documents are likely to be examined regularly. Understanding who the various user groups of financial information are, along with their purpose, are also important.

chapter

2

Principles and process of bookkeeping

In this chapter

- The accounting equation.
- The elements of the financial statements.
- Key accounts in financial statements.
- The process to prepare financial statements.
- Accounting systems.
- Computerised accounting.
- The general ledger and ledger accounting.
- The journal.

The accounting equation

Key Point

The accounting equation shows relationship between assets and liabilities in accounting system.

Definition

Business entity concept: A business is separate from its owners.

Any business always has:

- Assets – resources controlled
- Liabilities – amounts owed to third parties
- Capital – money introduced by owners

Assets
- Land and buildings
- Plant and machinery
- Motor vehicles
- Inventory
- Money in bank
- Receivables

=

Liabilities
- Payables
- Bank loan
- Bank overdraft
- Other payables (e.g. tax due to tax authorities)

+

Capital
- Amounts introduced to business by owner

- Elements change over time (e.g. when a sale occurs inventory will fall and money in bank-increase)

Assets
- $2,000 Land
- $3,000 Inventory
- $1,500 – Money in the bank
- Total $5,500

=

Liabilities
- $1,500 due to payables

+

Capital
- $4,000 capital from owner

Income, expenses and profit

- Businesses sell goods and services

Definition

- Income = amounts received for selling goods and services
- Expenses = amounts paid to provide those goods and services
- Profit = excess of income over expenditure. Added to owner's capital (or deducted if a loss)

Key Point

Every transaction has two effects (the dual aspect). This means that after each transaction the accounting equation will still balance.

Income
- Sales of goods/services

–

Expenses
- Cost of materials used
- Salaries
- Telephone charges
- Rent
- Light, heat and power
- Interest on bank loan

=

Profit
- Surplus of sales over expenses paid
- Can be negative – indicates loss

The elements of the financial statements

Financial position – shown in the statement of financial position **Statement of financial position** = a statement of assets, liabilities and equity at a certain point in time.	
Asset	A present economic resource controlled by the entity as a result of past events e.g. buildings, inventory, trade receivables.
Liability	A present obligation of the entity to transfer an economic resource as a result of past events e.g. bank loan or overdraft, trade payables.
Equity	The residual interest in the assets after deducting all the liabilities from the total assets. Also known as capital.
Financial performance – statement of profit or loss and other comprehensive income. **Statement of profit or loss and other comprehensive income.** = a summary of income and expenditure over a period of time.	
Income	Increases in assets, or decreases in liabilities, that result in increases in equity, other than those relating to contributions from the holders of equity claims.
Expense	Decreases in assets, or increases in liabilities, that result in decreases in equity, other than those relating to distributions to holders of equity claims.

Key accounts in financial statements

The financial statements are based upon the elements of the financial statements and are a development of the information expressed in the accounting equation.

The statement of profit or loss summarises the revenues earned and expenses incurred by an entity during an accounting period, usually one year.

Statement of financial position – a statement of assets, liabilities and capital as at a specific date or point in time.

Notes to the financial statements – additional explanation and clarification of amounts included in the financial statements.

Statement of profit or loss:

- Shows financial performance for business for one period of time (normally 12 months)
- Revenue = amounts obtained from selling goods and services
- Expenses = costs incurred in providing goods / services
- Profit = difference between revenue and expenses. It is transferred to the statement of financial position.

Key Point

The statement of profit or loss shows performance over a period of time; the statement of financial position shows position at one point in time.

Revenue

- Sales of goods/services less sales returns

–

Expenses

- Cost of goods sold
- Salaries
- Telephone
- Rent
- Light, heat and power
- Interest on bank loan, etc

=

Profit

- Surplus over expenses paid
- Can be negative – indicates 'loss'

Statement of financial position

- Shows overall financial position of business at a particular date in time
- Assets = something owned or controlled by the business
- Liabilities = amounts owed by business to third parties
- Assets and liabilities can be current or non-current
- Capital = owner's investment + (-) all profits (losses) to date – all drawings to date
- Drawings = amounts of cash withdrawn from the business by the owner.

Non-current assets	• Plant and machinery/ motor vehicles
+	
Current assets	• Inventory, receivables, cash
–	
Current liabilities	• Payables, bank overdraft
–	
Non-current liabilities	• Bank loan
=	
Capital	• Owner's money invested in business less drawings
+	
Profits	• Surpluses from previous years

- A **non-current asset** is an asset that is purchased for use within the business in the generation of revenues and profits over more than one accounting period, such as land and buildings, plant and machinery and motor vehicles.
- **Current assets** are assets that are expected to be converted into cash as part of the normal operating activities of the entity within twelve months of the accounting year end. They will include items such as inventories available for sale and receivables, which are amounts due from credit customers.
- A **non-current current liability** is a liability that is not required to be settled until at least twelve months after the accounting year end. An example of this is a long-term bank loan.
- A **current liability** is a liability that will be settled within twelve months following the accounting year end. Examples include payables, which are amounts owing to suppliers not yet paid and sales tax owing to the tax authorities.

The process to prepare financial statements

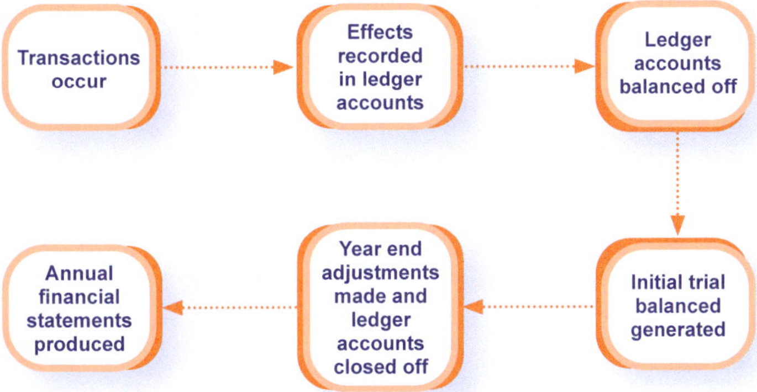

Accounting systems

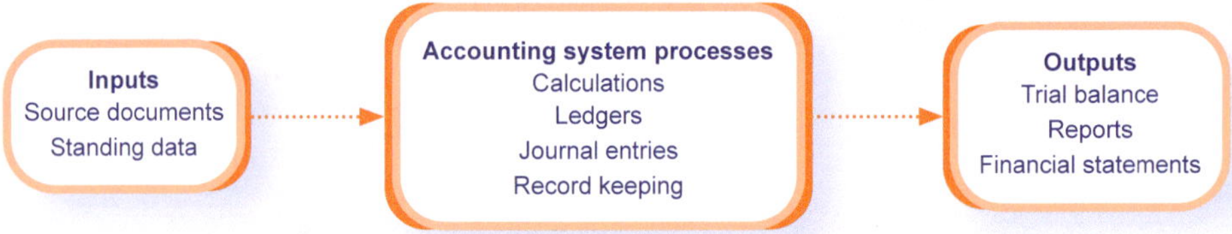

Computerised accounting

Computerised bookkeeping uses same principles as manual bookkeeping. Double entry still performed – although printouts unlikely to be in 'T' account format.

Advantages of computers	Disadvantages of computers
• Speed • Work from stored programs – needs fewer staff • Reliable – fewer mistakes than manual systems • Can be programmed to undertake complex decision making • Large amounts of data can be stored in very little space and retrieved quickly	• Lack of intelligence – cannot recognise errors or incomplete data • Relatively high initial costs • More difficult to amend computer programs than manual system • Makes organisation dependent on computer – more vulnerable to loss of resource • Can only make quantifiable not judgemental decisions

Cloud computing is access to software and data storage that is hosted on remote servers and is accessed via the internet. Cloud computing enables data and information stored to be accessed from any location at any time by multiple users if the user has an internet connection and can log in.

Cloud accounting is the application of cloud computing to accounting systems and processes.

Advantages of cloud accounting	Disadvantages of cloud accounting
• Ability to share and share data on demand • No maintenance or damage of physical server • Improved disaster recovery and data security	• Reliance upon the financial stability of cloud service provider • Risk of unauthorised access by service provider staff • Responsibility of service provider to comply with relevant law e.g. data protection

Cloud accounting applications

- A payroll bureau – to enable production of the payroll.
- An external accountant – to produce sales tax returns and the annual financial statements.
- Customers – to place orders and pay for goods ordered.

The general ledger and ledger accounting

Ledgers – key definitions

Definition

A ledger is a collection of ledger accounts, each account recording transactions of the same type.

- General ledger = holds all individual ledger accounts used to prepare the financial statements.
- Personal ledgers = receivables ledger and payables ledger, holding individual accounts for all receivables/payables.

General ledger

- Contains all individual accounts needed to record business transactions.
- Shows double entry recording of all transactions.

Double entry rules

Debit entries record:	**Credit entries record:**
↑ in assets	↓ in assets
↓ in liabilities	↑ in liabilities
Expenses Drawings	Income Injections of capital

DEBIT (increases)	CREDIT (increases)
Expenses (SP&L) **A**ssets (SOFP) **D**rawings/**D**ividends (SOFP)	**L**iabilities (SOFP) **I**ncome (SP&L) **C**apital (SOFP)

The Journal

Definition

A journal is a record containing details of non-routine double entry transactions.

Uses of journal

- Correction of errors
- Year-end adjustments (e.g. depreciation)
- Recording of significant transactions (e.g. non-current asset purchase).

Exam focus

Many examination questions focus on the double entry required for different accounting transactions. Ensure you can prepare entries as T accounts as well as journals. Even with multiple-choice questions, it can be useful to prepare working T accounts to check the double entry of different transactions.

Format of journal

				31 December 20X4
Reference	**Detail**	**General ledger ref.**	**Debit $**	**Credit $**
52	Depreciation charge on motor vehicles	GL78	7,800	
	Accum. depreciation on motor vehicles	GL54		7,800
	Year end depreciaition charge for motor vehicles			

Exam focus

If a question asks for a journal, be sure to provide the Dr, Cr and narrative explanation.

Exam focus

Questions dealing with the accounting equation and elements of the financial statements are highly likely to appear in exams. The components of a set of financial statements are also important as preparation of the financial statements is the key output of recording transactions.

chapter

3

Recording transactions

In this chapter

- Sales and purchases transactions.
- Recording bank and petty cash transactions.
- Trade and settlement discounts.
- Sales tax.

Sales and purchases transactions

	Cash transactions	Credit transactions
Sales	Dr Cash at bank Cr Sales Cr Sales tax	Dr Trade receivables Cr Sales Cr Sales tax
Purchases	Dr Purchases Dr Sales tax Cr Cash at bank	Dr Purchases Dr Sales tax Cr Trade payables
Sales returns (returns inwards)	Dr Sales returns Dr Sales tax Cr Cash at bank	Dr Sales returns Dr Sales tax Cr Trade receivables
Purchases (returns outwards)	Dr Cash at bank Cr Purchases returns Cr Sales tax	Dr Trade payables Cr Purchases returns Cr Sales tax

Recording purchases

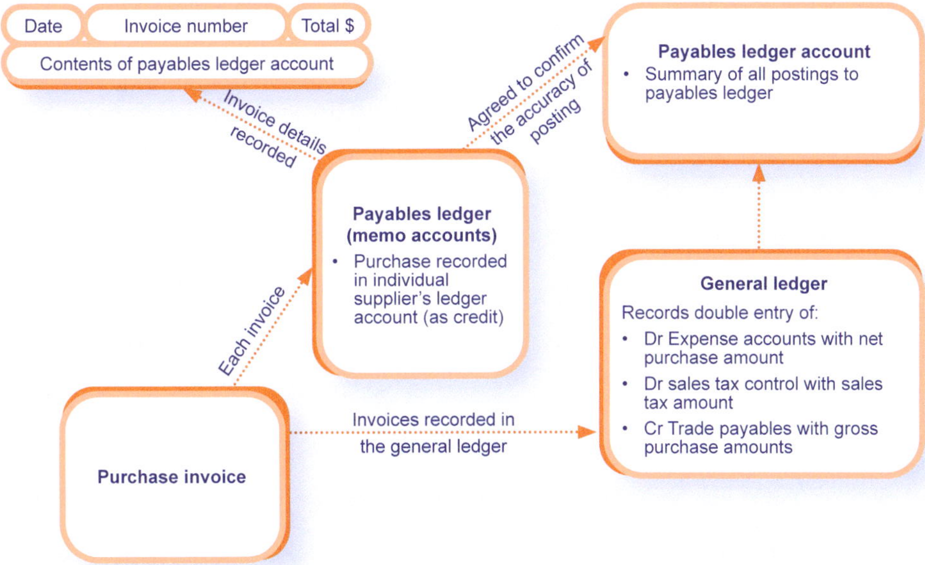

Recording purchase returns

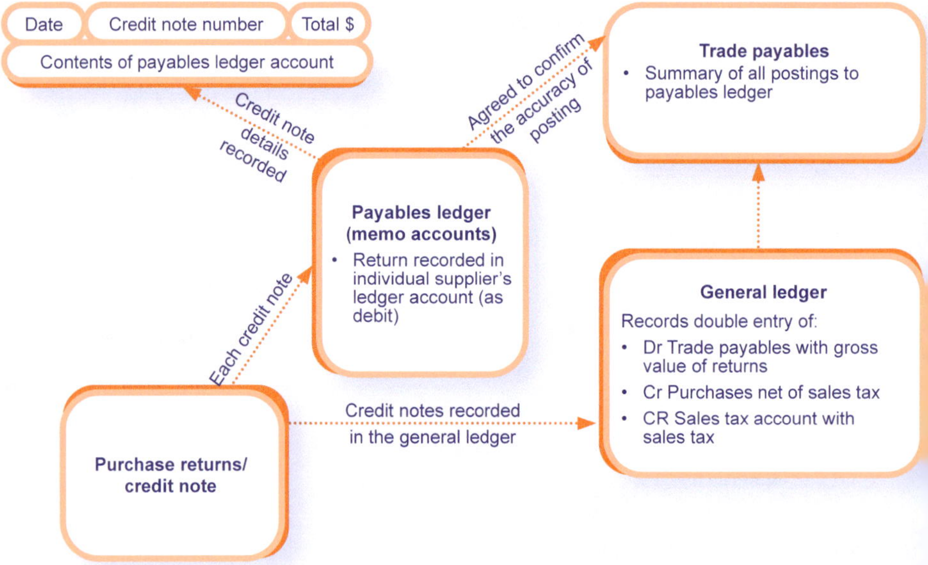

Recording a sales invoice

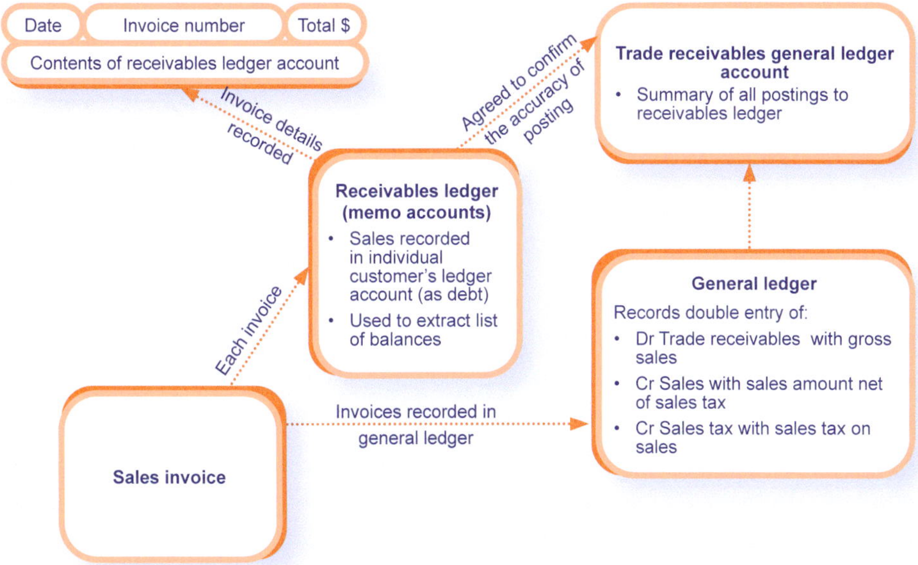

Recording sales returns

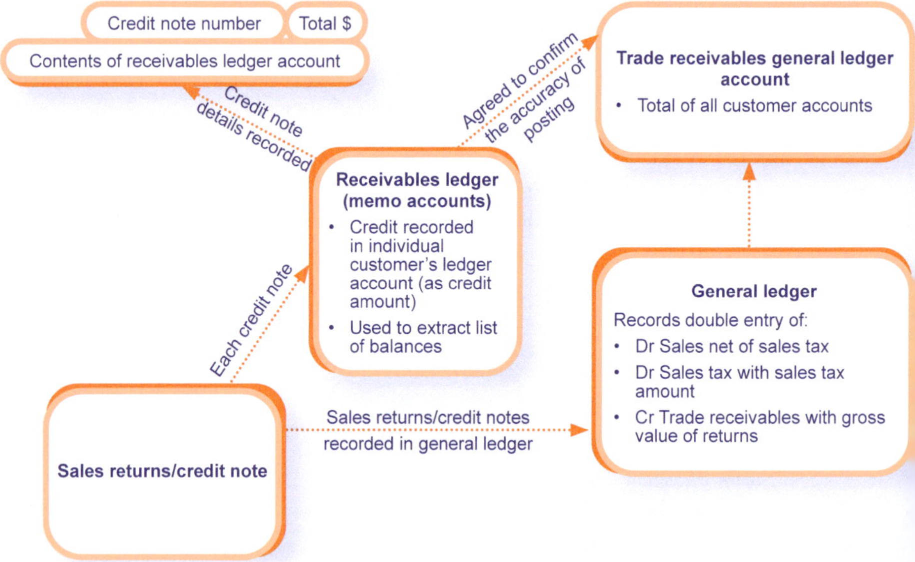

Recording bank and petty cash transactions

Recording receipts

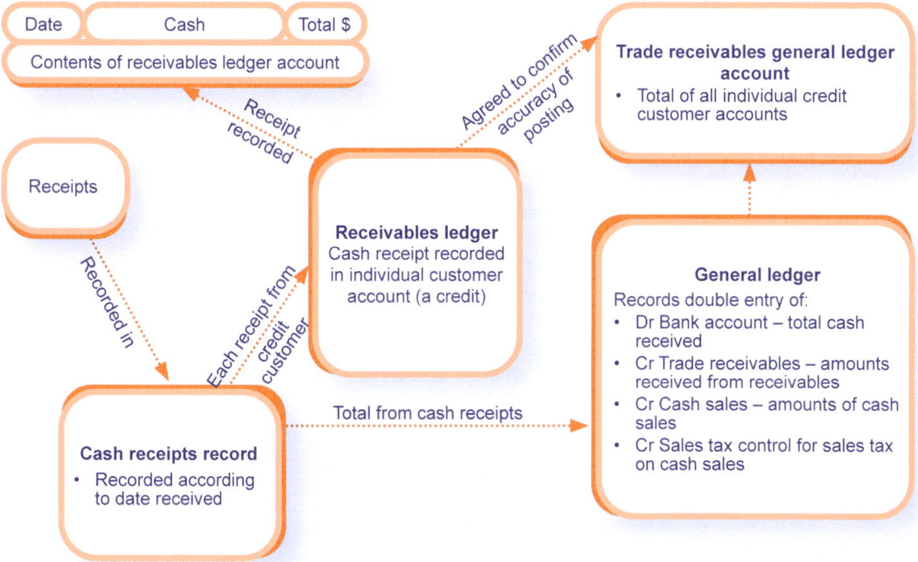

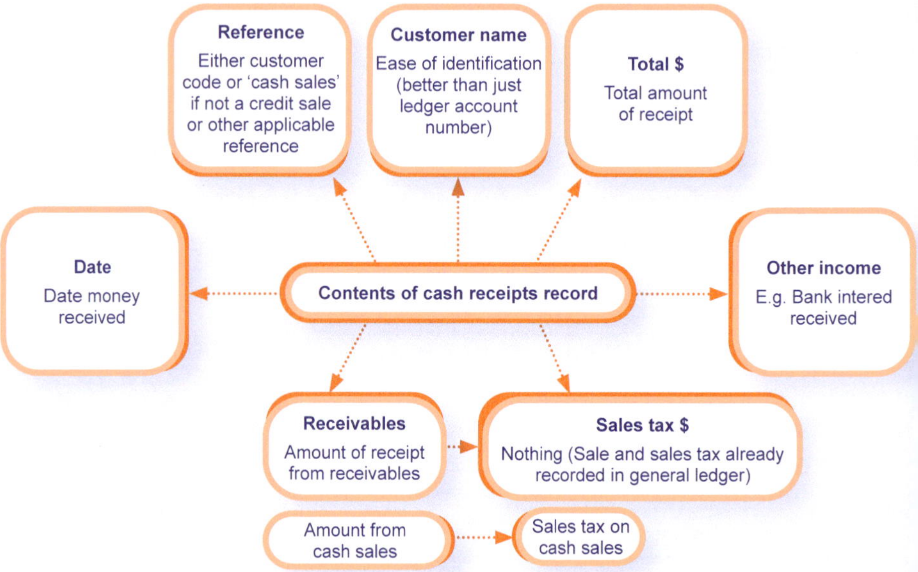

Note: Cash sales are assumed to be entered in the cash receipts record only, with the total split between the net sale value and sales tax amounts.

Cash payments

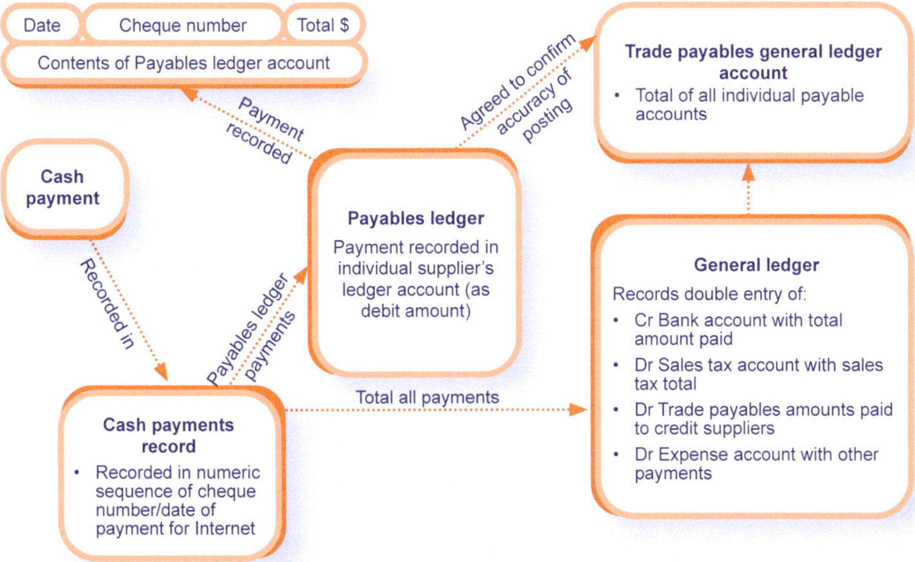

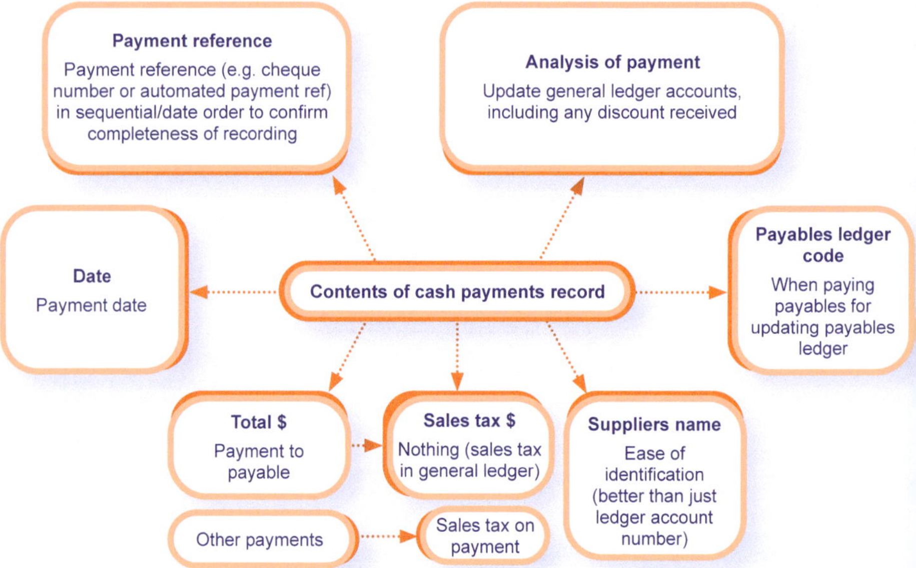

Note: Sales tax is only accounted for on payments not already in the general ledger. Invoices recorded in the general ledger will already have sales tax accounted for there.

Recording of petty cash

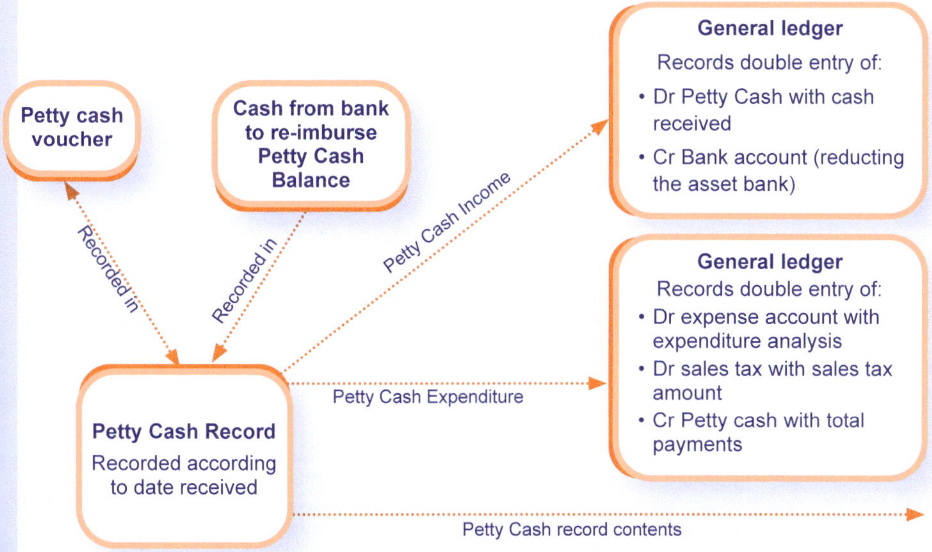

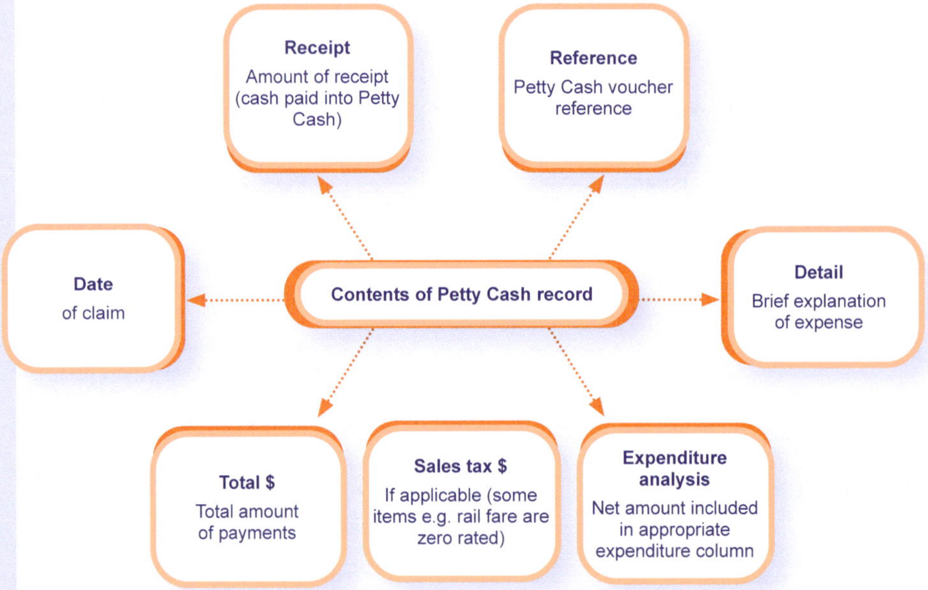
Receipt
Amount of receipt (cash paid into Petty Cash)
Reference
Petty Cash voucher reference
Date
of claim
Contents of Petty Cash record
Detail
Brief explanation of expense
Total $
Total amount of payments
Sales tax $
If applicable (some items e.g. rail fare are zero rated)
Expenditure analysis
Net amount included in appropriate expenditure column

The imprest system

Definition

An imprest system is one where, at any point in time, the sum of the cash held and the values of the vouchers raised in the period will equal a predetermined amount (the float or imprest amount).

- Float is set at a level thought sufficient to cover everyday expenses over a period (e.g. one week).
- Money taken out of petty cash for purchases is replaced by an authorised voucher detailing the transaction and attached to a receipt.

At any point in time:

CASH + VOUCHERS = FLOAT

If not, this may be due to:

- voucher made out wrongly and ≠ cash paid out
- cash stolen
- wrong amount of cash paid out
- At regular intervals, the vouchers are removed and totalled and an equal amount is withdrawn from the bank to replenish the float.

Trade and settlement discounts

Key Point

Always read questions carefully to identify if the transaction is subject to trade or settlement discount. Also – is the question stated from the perspective of the seller or the buyer?

Discounts

Discounts
Trade discounts
= discount given for ordering in large quantities as an incentive for regular customers
Reduction in selling price at point of sale
Record transaction at discounted price
Settlement discounts
= discount given for early payment of a debt (within a stated period of time)
Settlement discounts = discount given for early settlement of an amount due i.e. pay supplier within 7 days of invoice date
Seller to decide at point of sale whether settlement discount terms likely to be taken up by customer
If probable that settlement discount terms will be taken up by customer, deduct from price in arriving at invoice amount
If probable that settlement discount terms will not be taken up by customer, do not deduct from price in arriving at invoice amount
Adjust for any cash received in excess of receivable recorded (or of shortfall of cash received) against revenue
Purchaser decides whether to take advantage of settlement discount terms
If will do so, pay reduced amount and record discount received to clear payable previously recorded as follows:
Dr Trade payables
Cr Bank
Cr Discount received

Sales tax

Key Point

Always reads questions carefully to identify whether a business is (or is not) registered to account for sales tax. If it is registered, look to see whether monetary values are stated net of sales tax or are stated gross.

Definition

Taxable supplies are goods and services sold subject to sales tax.

Input tax is sales tax paid to suppliers which is suffered and paid on purchases by an entity.

Output tax is sales tax charged on sales by an entity and collected on behalf of the tax authority.

Credit transactions and sales tax

Credit transactions	Sales tax
Credit transaction = goods exchanged before payment made. However transactions are recorded as they occur therefore need payable/receivable accounts. **Credit purchase** 1 Purchase recorded and payable account set up showing amount due to supplier 2 Amount is later paid from bank. **Credit sale** 1 Sale recorded and receivable account set up showing amount due from receivable 2 Debtor pays invoice.	Applies to businesses registered for sales tax. **Sales** • Must add sales tax to sales made • Typical sales tax rate = 20% • Receivable amount recorded gross of sales tax • Sale recorded net of sales tax. **Purchases** • Sales tax charged on price by supplier • Payables amount is recorded gross of sales tax • Purchase recorded net of sales tax. **Net sales tax** Tax on sales X Tax on purchases (X) Tax payables to authorities X

Purchases and sales tax

Purchase	5,000
Sales tax	1,000
Total	6,000

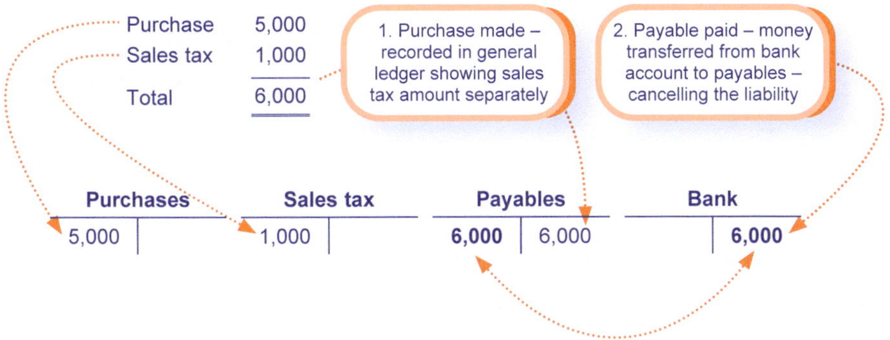

Sales and sales tax

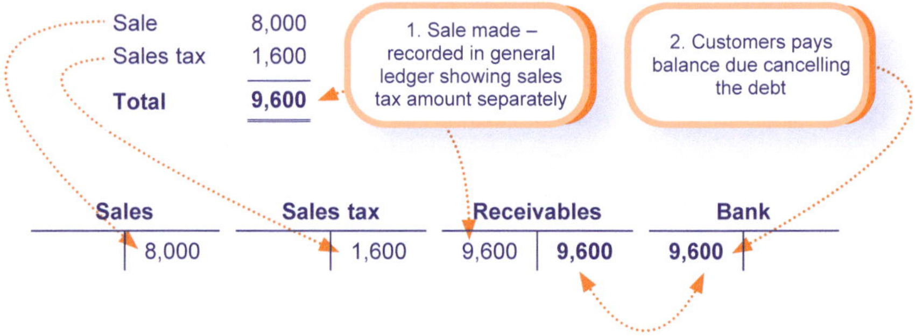

Net sales tax

- Calculated regularly (e.g. every 1 or 3 months)
- Excess of sales tax charged over incurred is paid to tax authorities

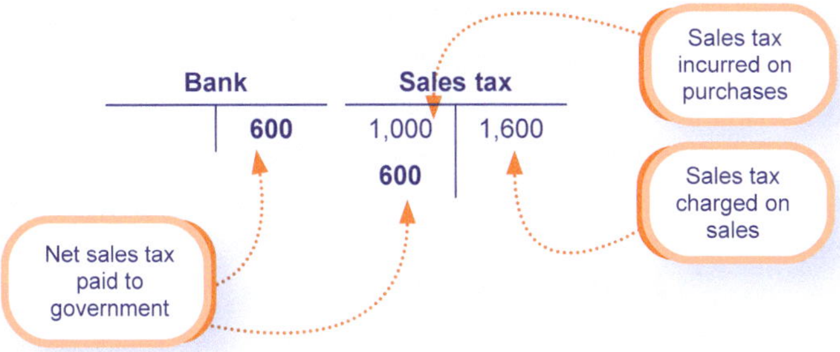

Exam focus

Sales tax is not relevant to all questions. Read the question carefully to decide whether it needs to be considered.

Exam focus

Questions dealing with recording transactions are a very important component of the ACCA FA2 syllabus and exam. Therefore, read questions carefully to identify the key characteristics of each transaction:

- Are you dealing with things from the perspective of the buyer or the seller?
- Is the transaction subject to trade or early settlement discount?
- Is the transaction subject to sales tax?
- Is the transaction stated before or after discounts and/or sales tax have been accounted for as appropriate?

chapter

4

Inventory

In this chapter

- Valuation of inventory.
- Cost v NRV.
- Inventory valuation methods.
- Accounting for inventory.

Valuation of inventory

Inventory

Finished goods: goods purchased ready for sale

Valuation per IAS 2 Inventories and stated at the lower of:

Cost

Expenditure to bring item to present location and condition:

- purchase price
- transport and handling costs
- less trade discounts

Net realisable value (NRV)

Selling price	X
Less: trade discounts	(X)
Less: further costs to completion	(X)
Less: marketing and selling expenses	(X)
NRV	X

Key Point

When applying the cost v NRV rule to inventories, each line of goods should be considered individually. Some lines will therefore be valued at cost and others at NRV.

Cost v NRV

Valuation options are:

Inventory item	Cost	Selling price	Costs to achieve sale	NRV	Inventory value
A	$2,000	$3,500	nil	$3,500	$2,000
B	$500	$600	$110	$490	$490
C	$1,500	$2,500	$800	$1,700	$1,500
D	$1,000	$1,500	$600	$900	$900

Exam focus

The examiner frequently states in his examiner's reports that students do not know the components of cost and NRV. You MUST learn these and be ready to apply them.

Inventory valuation methods

- Identical products often purchased at different times at different costs → in order to value inventory need to make assumption as to how goods move.
- Method must give good approximation of true cost of inventory.

Valuation methods

FIFO (first in first out)

Assumes inventory purchased first is sold first

AVCO (average cost)

Inventory valued at average of all purchase prices.
May be calculated as:

- Periodic weighted average
- Continuous weighted average

e.g

Example

		Units	$/unit
1 June	Purchases	100	5
3 June	Sale	10	
4 June	Purchases	200	6
5 June	Sale	170	

FIFO

Purchases	300	units	The 120 units of closing inventory are assumed to be part of the 4th June purchase.
Sales	(180)	units	
Closing inventory	120	units	120 units @ $6 = $720

AVCO – periodic weighted average

This method does not consider dates of purchase and sale, instead assuming that all transactions are completed on the last day of the period.

Purchases	$	Closing inventory:
100 units @ $5	500	
200 units @ $6	1,200	
300 units	1,700	120 units @ $5.67 = $680

Average $1,700/300 units = $5.67

AVCO – continuous weighted average

This method does consider dates of purchase and sale, with the average price updated after each transaction.

		Units	$/unit	Value
1 June	Purchase	100	5	500
3 June	Sale	(10)	5	(50)
		90		450
4 June	Purchase	200	6	1,200
		290		1,650
5 June	Sale	(170)	$1,650/290 = $5.69	(967)
Closing inventory		120		683

Accounting for inventory

- During year, inventory purchases always Dr Purchases Cr PLCA
- At end of year, adjustments take place as below

Statement of financial position 31.12.X1 (Extract)

	$	$
Non-current assets		
Plant	$	
Vehicles	$	
		$
Current assets		
Inventory	$	
Receivables	$	
Cash	$	

Statement of profit or loss 31.12.X2

	$	$
Sales		$
Cost of goods sold		
Opening inventory	$	
Purchases	$	
	$	
Closing inventory	$	
		$
Gross profit		$

Statement of financial position 31.12.X2 (Extract)

	$	$
Non-current assets		
Plant	$	
Vehicle	$	
		$
Current assets		
Inventory	$	
Receivables	$	
Cash	$	

Double-entry: Opening inventory	
Dr: Opening inventory SPL	$X
Cr Opening inventory SOFP	$X

Double-entry: Closing inventory	
Dr: Closing inventory SOFP	$X
Cr Closing inventory SPL	$X

chapter

5

Non-current assets

In this chapter

- Asset expenditure and expense.
- Non-current assets – key points.
- Accounting for non-current assets.
- Depreciation overview.
- Accounting for depreciation.
- Changes in depreciation.
- Disposals of non-current assets.
- Disposal and part exchange.
- Asset register.
- Asset counts.

Asset expenditure and expense

Expense	Asset expenditure
• Relates to one accounting period. • Is matched against revenue generated in that accounting period. • Example = inventory purchased for resale is matched to the sale of the inventory in the statement of profit or loss.	• Relates to more than one accounting period. • Is matched against the accounting periods when the asset expenditure generates income by way of depreciation. • Example = a computer with a useful economic life of 3 years is depreciated over 3 years.

Definition

Asset expenditure is expenditure on non-current assets.

Non-current assets – key points

Assets

Current assets
- Assets which will either be converted into cash within the next 12 months, or
- Will be consumed within the entity's normal operating cycle.

Examples: inventory, receivables, cash

Non-current assets
Assets which are purchased for continuing use within the business in the generation of profits over more than one accounting period.

Tangible non-current assets
Assets which can be physically touched, e.g. property, machines, vehicles.

Statement of financial position presentation
Typically grouped into categories, e.g.:
- Land and buildings
- Fixtures and fittings
- Motor vehicles.

Exam focus

Non-current assets are very examinable within multiple choice, short-form and longer questions. You must get to grips with this chapter.

Accounting for non-current assets

Acquire non-current asset

↓

Depreciate

↓

Dispose

Record at cost:

- Dr Non-current asset
- Cr Cash / payables

Cost includes all costs directly attributable to bringing the asset to the location and condition necessary for use:

- Purchase price of asset
- Delivery costs
- Site preparation
- Installation and assembly
- Associated professional fees

Sales tax is generally recoverable:

- Dr Non-current asset net cost
- Dr Sales tax account sales tax
- Cr Cash / payable gross cost

Sales tax on motor vehicles may not be recoverable. Therefore it becomes part of the cost of the asset.

Depreciation overview

Depreciation

Definition
Measure of cost of the economic benefits of the non-current asset that have been **consumed** during the period

Overall concept
Aim of depreciation: asset depreciated to residual value over estimated useful life

Residual value =
Estimated disposal proceeds from asset at end of useful life

Useful life =
Length of time business intends to use the asset

Freehold land
Has an infinite useful life and so is not depreciated

Non-current assets 'consumed' – lose value – by

- Use
- Passing of time e.g. lease
- Obsolescence – technological change
- Depletion – extraction of material from quarry

Types of

Straight line
Benefits from asset arise evenly over life therefore cost also spread evenly over life

$$\text{Annual charge} = \frac{(\text{Cost} - \text{residual value})}{\text{Useful life}}$$

Reducing balance
Assumes asset used more in earlier years hence depreciation charge higher in those early years

Charge this year = Carrying amount b/f x Depreciation %

e.g

Example

Straight line

Asset cost = $9,000

Useful life = 6 years

Residual value = $3,000

Depreciation = $1,000 pa

= (9,000-3,000) / 6 years

e.g

Example

Reducing balance

Asset CV b/f = $6,000

Depreciation rate = 25% pa

Depreciation = 6,000 x 25% = $1,500

CV c/f = $4,500

Accounting for depreciation

Accounting options

Charge a full year's depreciation in year of purchase, then none in year of sale.

Charge depreciation for each month the asset is used by the entity (pro-rata depreciation).

Depreciation double entry:

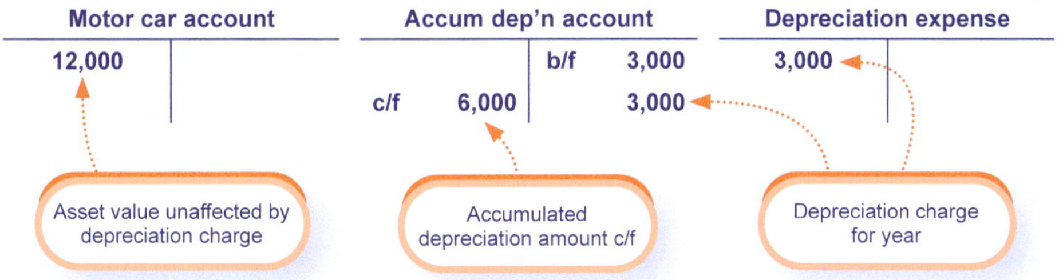

Asset value therefore:

Cost – Accumulated depreciation = Carrying amount

12,000 – 6,000 = 6,000

Accounting entries

Basic accounting entry is:

Dr Depreciation expense
(statement of profit or loss)

Cr Accumulated depreciation
(statement of financial position)

Exam focus

Note the accumulated depreciation account is also called the provision for depreciation account in some texts / questions.

Financial statements presentation

	Cost	Accum dep,n	CA
Motor vehicles	12,000	(6,000)	6,000
Plant	32,000	(18,000)	14,000
Total	44,000	(24,000)	20,000

- Cost, accumulated depreciation and carrying amount for each class of non-current asset are given either on the face of the statement of financial position or in a note to the accounts.
- A single depreciation expense account is listed in the statement of profit or loss.

Changes in depreciation

Change in useful life

- Write off remaining CA over remaining useful life.

Change in method of depreciation

- Only change if the new method will show a fairer presentation in the accounts.
- If change, write off the carrying amount over the remaining useful life using the new method.

Disposals of non-current assets

1 Transfer cost to disposals account.

2 Transfer accumulated depreciation to disposals account.

3 Enter sale proceeds into cash book and disposals account.

4 Find balance on disposals account.

- Profit = Dr Disposals / Cr Statement of profit or loss
- Loss = Dr Statement of profit or loss / Cr Disposals.

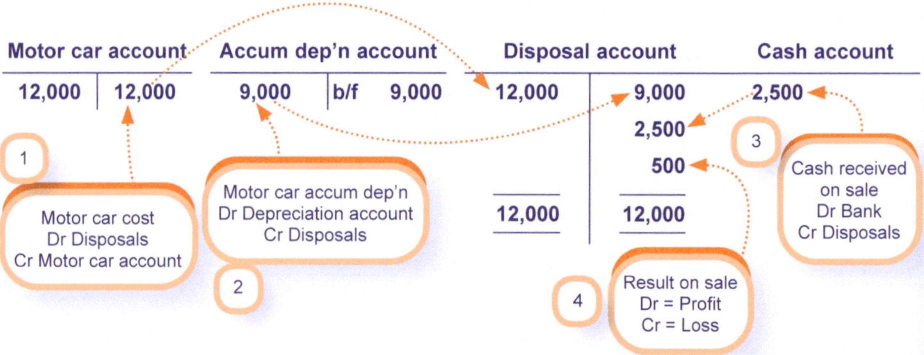

Key Point

If a non-current asset is 'scrapped', disposal proceeds are nil.

Disposal and part exchange

Situation where old asset is sold in part payment for new asset.

1 Transfer cost to disposals account (as disposal above – not shown on diagram below).

2 Transfer accumulated depreciation to disposals account (as disposal above – not shown on diagram below).

3 Enter purchase of new motor car as Dr Asset account (with full value) and Cr Cash book (with amount paid) and Cr Disposal account (with part exchange proceeds).

4 Find balance on disposals account

- Profit = Dr Disposals / Cr Statement of profit or loss
- Loss = Dr Statement of profit or loss / Cr Disposals.

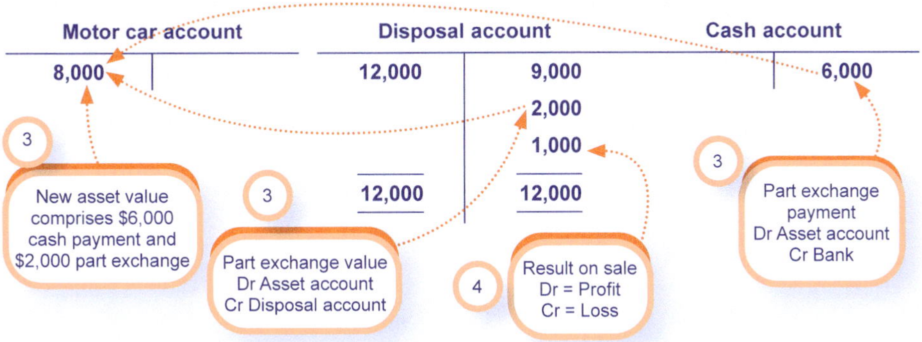

Exam focus

Many examination questions focus on calculation of depreciation and the profit/loss on sale. Ensure you are happy with the double entry for these calculations.

Asset register

Definition

A collection of records, one for each asset, carrying detailed information about each asset.

Example of information contained in register:

Asset number	Descrip-tion	Location	Supplier ref	Useful life	Dep'n method	Cost $	Scrap value $	Accum Dep'n b/f $	CA $	Date of disposal	Disposal proceeds $

Non-current asset register should be agreed to the general ledger monthly/annually. Acts as a control over completeness of the general ledger.

Asset counts

Definition

The inspection of assets owned by the business to check the accuracy and validity of entries in the asset register.

Procedure	Procedure for errors
1 List assets from the asset register. 2 Locate each asset – check against list – and determine condition. 3 Mark asset as counted (e.g. attach a coloured sticker). 4 Identify assets not marked as counted. 5 Identify any missing items from list.	**Non-current asset missing** • Remove asset from the asset register. **Non-current assets not in register** • Add to register – but at zero cost. • Likely that the asset was mis-categorised as revenue expenditure in the past.

chapter

6

Accruals and prepayments

In this chapter

- Accruals.
- Prepayments.
- Deferred income.
- Income received in arrears.
- Statement of financial position presentation.

Accruals

An accrual is an item of expense that has been incurred during the accounting period but not paid at the end of that accounting period.

Determine the amount of accrual as follows:

Double entry for accrual is:

Dr Expense account (in this case rent account)

Cr Accruals account on statement of financial position

Rent expense

Bank	**8,000**	**b/f**	**500**
Bank	**8,000**	**inc. stat.**	**20,000**
c/f	**4,500**		
	20,500		**20,500**

1. Find opening accrual from last year's trial balance
2. Record cash payments during period
3. Enter correct charge to statement of profit or loss
4. Find total on account (in this case credits > debits) before finding c/f balance
5. Calculate accrual as balance on account

Steps 3 and 5 may be reversed depending on the question: you may be given (or be able to calculate) the c/f accrual and so find the statement of profit or loss charge as a balancing figure.

Prepayments

Definition

A prepayment is an item of expense which has been paid during the current accounting period but will not be incurred until the next accounting period.

Determine amount of prepayment as follows:

Insurance expense

b/f	1,000	Profit or loss	5,500
Bank	6,000	c/f	1,500
	7,000		7,000

1. Find opening prepayment (from trial balance)
2. Record cash payments during period
3. Calculate prepayment
4. Find total on account (in this case debits > credits) before finding statement of profit or loss charge for the year
5. Find statement of profit or loss charge as balancing figure

Again, steps 3 and 5 may be reversed: you may be given (or be able to calculate) the statement of profit or loss charge for the year and so find the prepayment at the period end as a balancing figure.

Double entry for the prepayment is:

Dr Prepayment account (on statement of financial position)

Cr Expense account (in this case insurance)

Deferred income

Definition

Deferred income is income received in advance.

Accounting treatment is the opposite of expenses payable – as shown below:

Double entry for the rent received in advance is:

Dr Income account (in this case rent receivable)

Cr Deferred income account (a liability on the statement of financial position)

Note this is a liability because it is an amount owed by the business at the end of the year.

Rental income

Profit or loss	**12,000**	**b/f**	**1,000**
c/f	**1,000**	**Bank**	**12,000**
	13,000		**13,000**

1. Find opening deferred income from last year's trial balance
2. Record cash receipts during period
3. Enter statement of profit or loss rent receivable for the period
4. Find total on account (in this case credits > debits) before finding c/f balance
5. Calculate deferred income c/f

Income received in arrears

If income is received in arrears, it is received after the service it relates to is provided. This results in a period-end statement of financial position asset of income owed to the business.

The double entry for the income received in arrears is:

Dr Income due (or accrued income) account (on the statement of financial position)

Cr Income account (statement of profit or loss)

Interest income

b/f	**80**	**Bank**	**800**
Profit or loss	**790**	**c/f**	**70**
	870		**870**

1. Find opening asset from last year's trial balance
2. Record cash receipts during period
3. Calculate income due at the period end (accrued income)
4. Find total on account (in this case debits > credits) before finding statement of profit or loss receivable amount
5. Find statement of profit or loss receivable amount as balancing figure

Statement of financial position presentation

Prepayment	Shown under current assets
Accrual	Shown under current liabilities
Deferred income	Shown under current liabilities
Income received in arrears	Shown under current assets

Exam focus

Questions on accruals and prepayments are examined frequently. Ensure that you are familiar with the accounting entries dealing with these issues.

chapter

7

Receivables

In this chapter

- Trade receivables in the general ledger.
- Irrecoverable debts.
- Irrecoverable debts – accounting treatment.
- Allowance for receivables.
- Irrecoverable debts and allowance for receivables – summary.
- Financial statements presentation.

Trade receivables in the general ledger

The trade receivables' general ledger account normally includes the following entries:accounting period.

Trade receivables

	$		$
Balance b/f	X	Sales returns	X
Credit sales	X	Cash at bank	X
Bank – dishonoured cheques	X	Irrecoverable debts	X
Bank – refunds of credit balances	X	Contra with payables ledger	X
Interest charged	X	Balance c/f	X
	X		X
Balance b/f	X		

Irrecoverable debts

If a debt is considered to be uncollectible, it should be written off.

To write off an **irrecoverable** debt	If an **irrecoverable** debt is recovered
Dr irrecoverable debts expense account Cr Receivables	Dr Bank Cr irrecoverable debts recovered account

Total irrecoverable debts = **expense** in **SP&L**

Irrecoverable debts **do not appear** in the **statement of financial position** as they have already been deducted from the figure of receivables.

Irrecoverable debts – accounting treatment

Allowance for receivables

		b/f	**1,000**
c/f	**1,350**	**Irr. debts**	**350**
	1,350		**1,350**

1. Find opening allowance from last year's trial balance
2. Calculate cf amount c/f amount = specific allowance
3. Find total on account (in this case debits > credits)
4. Find balancing figure and transfer to irrecoverable debts account. Note the transfer = difference between opening and closing balances

Irrecoverable debts expense

Allowance	**350**		
Trade receivables	**150**	**Profit or loss**	**500**
	500		**500**

1. Transfer from allowance for receivables account
2. Write off specific irrecoverable debts
3. Balance account
4. Balancing figure transfer to statement of P&L

Allowance for receivables

Where a customer is known to be in financial difficulties and therefore the amount owing may not be recoverable, an allowance can be created. The debt remains in the ledger accounts, but the allowance is deducted from the figure of receivables in the statement of financial position.

Dr	Irrecoverable debts expense account
Cr	Allowance for receivables account

In the following period if there is a decrease in the allowance the double entry will be as follows:

Dr	Allowance for receivables account
Cr	Irrecoverable debts expense account

e.g

Example

Calculation of allowance for receivables

Smith's receivables allowance is $23,000 at the period end. Smith wishes to make a specific allowance for amounts of $1,200 owed by Jones and $700 owed by Morgan.

The allowance at the end of the last period was $2,100.

	$		$
Receivables balance	23,000		
Specific allowance			
Jones	(1,200)		1,200
Morgan	(700)		700
	21,000	=	
Total allowance			1,900
b/f allowance			(2,100)
Decrease in allowance			200
Dr Allowance for receivables	200		
Cr Irrecoverable debts expense	200		

Format of the allowance for receivables account

Allowance for receivables			
		Bal b/d (opening allowance)	X
SP&L (decrease in allowance)	X	SP&L (increase in allowance)	X
Bal c/d (closing allowance)	X		
	X		X

Irrecoverable debts and allowance for receivables – summary

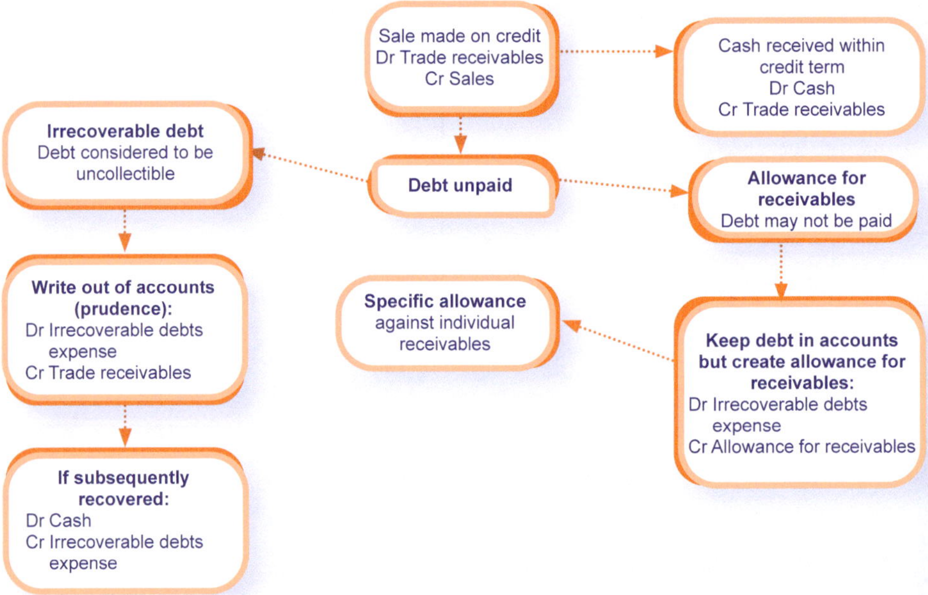

Financial statements presentation

Allowance for receivables
Deduct from receivables on statement of financial position
Irrecoverable debts expense
Shown in statement of profit or loss

Statement of financial position

The **total** allowance is deducted from the figure of receivables.

	20X6	20X7
	$	$
Current assets:		
Receivables (less irrecoverable debts written off)	(x)	(x)
Less:		
Allowance for receivables	(x)	(x)
	x	x

Statement of profit or loss and other comprehensive income

Only the **change** in the allowance for receivables is included in the statement of profit or loss, normally within the irrecoverable debts expense account. An increase in the allowance is treated as an expense. A reduction in the allowance is treated as either income or a negative expense.

Exam focus

You will be required to calculate any of the figures regarding the irrecoverable debts or allowance for receivables figure.

chapter

8

Payables and provisions

In this chapter

- Trade payables in the general ledger.
- Definitions.
- Liabilities and provisions.

Trade payables in the general ledger

The trade payables' general ledger account may include any of the following entries:

Trade payables

Cash at bank	X	Balance b/f	X
Purchases returns	X	Credit purchases	X
Early settlement discounts received	X	Interest on overdue accounts	X
Contra with receivables' ledger	X		
Balance c/f	X		
	X		X
		Balance b/f	X

Definitions

A **liability** is an obligation to transfer economic benefits as a result of past transactions or events.

A **current liability** is an item that is due to be paid within one year. Current liabilities include rade payables, amounts collected on behalf of the tax authorities and accruals.

A **non-current liability** is an item that is due to be paid after more than one year where there is no right for the other party to demand more immediate payment. A good example of this is a long-term bank loan.

A **provision** is a liability of uncertain timing and/or amount.

Liabilities and provisions

Liability		Provision
Liability An obligation to transfer economic benefits as a result of past transactions or events	**Definition**	**Provision** A liability of uncertain timing or amount
Dr Purchases Cr Trade payables with credit purchase or Dr Bank Cr Loan account with non-current loan	**Accounting treatment**	Dr Expense account Cr Provisions (on statement of financial position)
As soon as liability incurred e.g. inventory purchased or loan received from bank	**Recognised**	ONLY recognised when: • Entity has presented obligation (legal or constructive) in response to past event • Probable that transfer of economic benefits needed to settle obligation and • Reliable estimate can be made of amount
	Measures	• At best estimate • Using expected values (example on next page)
Payables: Shown under current liabilities. Loan: Shown under current/non-current liabilities	**Statement of financial position presentation**	Long-term: Shown under non-current liabilities as provisions: Short term: shown under current liabilties under Provisions

- **Legal obligation =** an obligation that is the result of a contract or legislation or other operation of law.
- **Constructive obligation =** an obligation that arises because an entiry has indicated, and so created and expectation, that will meet obligations not legally required of it.

Exam focus

Questions on these areas tend to focus on the different methods of the accounting treatment of liabilities and provisions – good areas therefore to revise.

Key Point

If part of a loan is due for repayment within a year, it is a current liability. The balance is a non-current liability.

Example

Measurement of provision using expected values

A business provides one-year warranties for the washing machines that it manufactures and sells. There is an 80% chance that no repairs will be needed to a washing machine within the first year; a 15% chance that minor repairs will be needed and a 5% chance that major repairs will be needed. If all machines required minor repairs the cost would be $100,000. If all machines required major repairs the cost would be $200,000. What provision should be made?

Solution

		$
Expected cost of minor repairs	15% x $100,000	15,000
Expected cost of major repairs	5% x $200,000	10,000
Provision required		25,000

chapter

9

Reconciliations

In this chapter

- Need for a bank reconciliation.
- Reasons for differences.
- Dishonoured cheques.
- Format of bank reconciliation.
- Preparing a bank reconciliation.
- Supplier statement reconciliations.

Need for a bank reconciliation

A bank reconciliation:

- Checks the accuracy of the bank ledger account by agreeing the balance to an independent source
- Identifies errors (in the bank ledger account and made by the bank)
- Explains the difference between the balance on the bank ledger account and the balance on the bank statement.

Reasons for differences

Reasons for differences

Items on bank statement but not in bank ledger (unrecorded differences)

Items that the business does not know about until the bank statement arrives:

- Bank charges
- Bank interest
- Direct debits/credits
- Dishonoured cheques
- Standing order

Items in bank ledger but not in bank statement (timing differences)

Unpresented (uncleared) cheques =

cheques written by the business but either not yet paid in or not yet cleared by the bank

Outstanding (uncleared) deposits =

amounts paid into the bank by the business which have not yet gone through the bank's clearing system

Dishonoured cheques

Definition

Dishonoured cheques are cheques that the drawer's bank refuses to honour – normally because the drawer's bank account is overdrawn.

Customer therefore still owes amount due.

Double entry for returned cheque is:

Dr Trade receivables (and receivable's personal account in the receivables ledger)

Cr Bank

Format of bank reconciliation

Bank ledger account

Balance b/d	X		
Bank interest (received)	X	Bank interest (paid)	X
Direct credit	X	Direct debit	X
		Bank charges	X
		Standing order	X
		Dishonoured cheques	X
		Balance c/d	X
	X		X
Balance b/d	Y		

Bank reconciliation	**$**
Balance on the bank statement	X
Less: unpresented cheques	(X)
Add: outstanding deposits	X
Revised bank balance	Y

Preparing a bank reconciliation

1 Set out a proforma bank ledger account and bank reconciliation.

2 Tick the bank statement to the detailed listing of bank ledger receipts and payments. Update for items included in the bank statement but not entered in the general ledger. In the exam this is achieved by making adjustments directly to the bank ledger account.

3 Tick the cash received and cheque payments detailed listing of bank ledger receipts and payments to the bank statement to identify unpresented cheques and outstanding deposits. Adjust for these in the bank reconciliation proforma.

4 Balance the bank ledger account and agree the balance to the completed bank reconciliation.

5 The revised balance is shown in the statement of financial position.

Exam focus

Bank reconciliation questions tend to include similar adjustments. Make sure you are familiar with them. Deal with these common adjustments first in a bank reconciliation question and leave any trickier points until later.

Supplier statement reconciliations

A monthly statement often sent by suppliers which lists movements on the account. A suppliers' statement reconciliation can then be performed as an additional check that all transactions have been recorded.

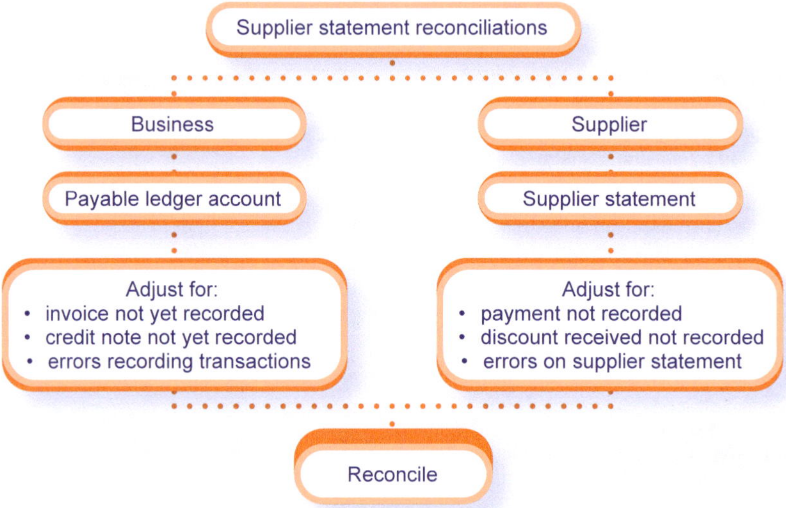

Exam focus

Questions dealing with reconciliations may require you to derive the relevant general ledger account balance, or to calculate the statement balance.

chapter

10

Trial balance and correction of errors

In this chapter

- Reasons for producing a trial balance.
- Limitations of a trial balance.
- Producing a trial balance.
- Errors not identified by a trial balance.
- Correction of errors not identified by a trial balance.
- Errors identified by a trial balance in a manual accounting system.
- The suspense account.
- Correction of errors involving a suspense account.

Reasons for producing a trial balance

- Check that double entry procedures have been followed: total debits should = total credits
- Starting point for the preparation of statement of profit or loss and statement of financial position
- Shows current balances on all accounts – useful for management
- Helps identify errors in accounting records.

Definition

The trial balance is a list of balances extracted from the general ledger.

Limitations of a trial balance

- Only identifies some errors
- Does not identify where errors have been made or what they are.

Producing a trial balance

1. Balance all accounts in general ledger
2. List balances of all accounts separating debit and credit balances as shown on right (some headings e.g. assets will have more than one entry in a 'real' trial balance)
3. Total the debits and credits – they should be the same
4. Where the total debits do not equal the total credits, investigate and find reason(s) for discrepancy.

The process noted above explains the procedures to produce a trial balance. In a computerised accounting system, this would normally be produced automatically when required.

Balances on a trial balance

Trial balance

	Dr	Cr
Assets	$	
Liabilities		$
Capital		$
Drawings (from capital)	$	
Income (sales)		$
Discounts received		$
Purchase returns		$
Expenses	$	
Sales returns	$	
Irrecoverable debts	$	
Should be the same	**Total**	**Total**

Errors not identified by a trial balance

Key Point

The error examples below may occur in both computerised and manual accounting systems as there will be an equal value of debits and credits recorded in the general ledger.

Error	Example
Error of commission Correct amount entered into correct category of account but wrong account.	The purchase of a motor vehicle recorded in the premises account.
Error of principle Correct amount entered but in the wrong 'class' of account.	Amount for a motor vehicle repair entered as a debit in the motor vehicle account (treating an expense as an asset addition).
Error of complete omission A transaction has not been recorded at all.	Purchase invoice not entered into the general ledger accounts.
Compensating errors One error coincidentally cancelled by another of the same amount.	A cash sale of $30 is accidentally debited to cash as $3 and depreciation of $27 is debited to depreciation expense but not credited to accumulated depreciation.
Original entry errors: debit and credit wrong The debit and credit entries are equal but for the wrong amount.	A cash purchase of $90 is entered into the purchases and cash accounts as $19.
Error of complete reversal The double entry is correct in every respect other than the debit and credit are posted the wrong way round.	Payment of an electricity bill is recorded as a credit to electricity expense and a debit to bank.

Correction of errors not identified by a trial balance

The best approach is to consider:

1 What double entry should have been posted (i.e. what is the correct double entry to record the transaction)? (SHOULD DO)
2 What double entry was posted? (DID DO)
3 What entry is therefore required to move from the entry that was posted to the entry that should have been posted? (TO CORRECT)

e.g **Example**

A cash purchase of $90 is entered into the purchases and cash accounts as $19.

Should do	Did do	To correct
Dr Purchases $90 Cr Cash $90	Dr Purchases $19 Cr Cash $19	Dr Purchases $71 Cr Cash $71 To record the purchases previously unrecorded

The correction journal should always have an equal debit and credit.

Errors identified by a trial balance in a manual accounting system

Errors in producing the trial balance

- An account is balanced incorrectly meaning that the amount shown in the trial balance is wrong.
- An account is completely omitted from the trial balance.
- A debit balance is placed in the credit column or vice versa.
- Note that the ACCA FA2 syllabus and exam presumes that computerised accounting systems are used to record transactions. Therefore, errors that would result in recording an unequal value of debits and credits in the general ledger are unlikely to occur.

Errors identified by the trial balance

Error	Example
Error of partial omission Either the debit or credit entry has not been posted to the accounts.	The owner injects capital into the business and the only entry is to debit cash.
Original entry errors: either debit or credit wrong One entry is for the correct amount, but the other is for a different amount.	Rental income of $450 is credited correctly but the debit entry is made for $45.
Transposition error Arises where two numbers within a balance are reversed when entering the transaction into the ledgers. This normally only occurs on one side of the entry. If it occurs on both, the TB will not identify the error.	Drawings of $120 are correctly recorded in the bank ledger but recorded as $210 in the drawings ledger.
Double debit or double credit A transaction is recorded as two debits or two credits.	A cash payment for motor expenses is debited to both the cash and motor expense accounts. No credit entry is made.

The suspense account

Definition

The suspense account is a multi-purpose account used to:

- In a computerised accounting system, the suspense account may be used as a temporary account to record one part of a transaction whilst seeking further information or clarification of that transaction. Upon receiving that information, the suspense account can be cleared with the the transaction fully and correctly recorded.
- Used in a manual accounting system when debits and credits in the trial balance are not equal.

Key Point

- The suspense account requires clearing prior to preparation of the financial statements.

Exam focus

Remember that not all errors involve the suspense account – in an exam question, the majority will probably not.

Correction of errors involving a suspense account

Errors in producing the trial balance

Error	Correction	Example
An account is balanced incorrectly meaning that the amount shown in the trial balance is wrong.	Adjust the amount in the trial balance to be correct and send the opposite entry to the suspense account.	A cash balance of $560 has been wrongly extracted from the general ledger and listed in the trial balance. The balance should be $580. ↓ Increase the cash balance in the TB by $20 (a debit) and credit suspense with $20.
An account is completely omitted from the trial balance.	Insert the account in the trial balance and send the opposite entry to the suspense account.	Accruals of $200 have been omitted from the TB. ↓ Add the accruals balance to the credit side of the TB and debit suspense with $200.
A debit balance is placed in the credit column or vice versa.	Show the balance in the correct column of the TB and send double the amount of the balance to suspense.	Sales of $23,000 are shown in the debit column of the TB. ↓ Move to the credit column (by crediting $46,000) and debit suspense with $46,000.

Errors identified by the trial balance

- Again the best approach is the 'should do', 'did do', 'to correct' approach.
- When considering 'did do', there will not be an equal debit and credit.
- You may find it helpful to think about the suspense account arising here to make the entries equal.
- The correction journal will then always involve the reversal of any 'did do' suspense entry.
- The correction journal should always include equal debits and credits.

e.g

Example

An injection of capital of $450 was recorded correctly in the capital account but as $540 in the bank ledger.

Should do	Did do	To correct
Dr Bank $450 Cr Capital $450	Dr Bank $540 Cr Capital $450 (Cr Suspense $90)	Dr Suspense $90 Cr Bank $90 To reverse the extra amount debited to bank.

Exam focus

Some of the more challenging examination questions involve the clearing of a suspense account balance. Try to follow the procedures outlined above for each error found, being very careful to get the debits and credits of the correcting entry right. Always deal with the easiest corrections first.

chapter

11

Preparing the financial statements

In this chapter

- Approach to preparing the financial statements.
- Compilation of the financial statements.

Approach to preparing the financial statements

Statement of profit or loss	Statement of financial position
1 Identify revenue and expense accounts in the general ledger.	1 Identify asset and liability accounts in the general ledger.
2 Find balances on individual accounts.	2 Find balances on individual accounts.
3 Transfer balances to statement of profit or loss.	3 Transfer balances to the statement of financial position.

- Financial statements should be prepared regularly as required.
- Prepared annually for filing and taxation purposes.

Definition

Trading account = sales less cost of goods sold to give gross profit.

Exam focus

You must learn the format of the statement of profit or loss and statement of financial position.

Compilation of the financial statements

Statement of profit or loss

	$	**$**
Sales		$
Costs of goods sold		
Opening inventory	$	
Purchases	$	
	$	
Closing inventory	($)	
		($)
Gross profit		$
Expenses		
Rent	$	
Electricity	$	
Etc.	$	
		($)
Net profit		$

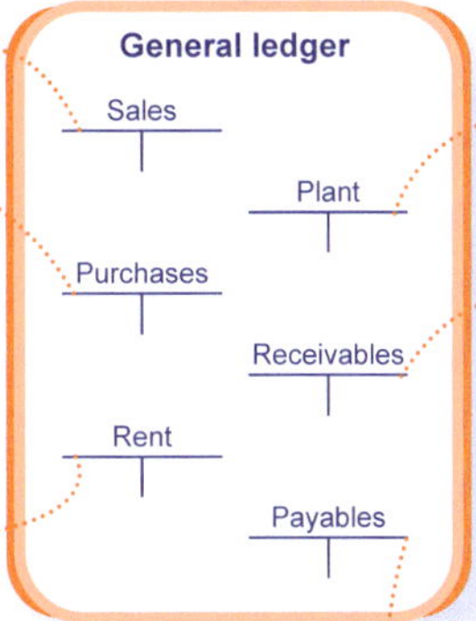

Statement of financial position

Non-current assets	**$**	**$**
Plant	$	
Vehicles	$	
		$
Current assets		
Inventory	$	
Receivables	$	
Cash	$	
		$
Total assets		$
Capital	$	
Add: profit	$	
Less: drawings	($)	
Non-current liabilities		$
Bank loan		$
Current liabilities		
Payables	$	
Sales tax owing	$	
Total capital and liabilities		$
		$

Note not all general ledger accounts shown

Exam focus

It is likely that your exam may include questions testing your knowledge of the compilation and format of the financial statements. Ensure that you are familiar with the format of the financial statements.

chapter

12

Sole trader accounts

In this chapter

- Preparation of the financial statements.
- Common year-end adjustments.
- Closing the books.

Preparation of the financial statements

Final accounts may be prepared from a trial balance

Preparation from a trial balance

You may be provided with a trial balance and list of year-end adjustments. You should:

1 Work out the double entries for the adjustments.

2 Work out the effect of these entries on the balances in the TB.

3 Slot the adjusted balances into the statement of financial position and statement of profit or loss.

The following pages summarise the common year-end adjustments.

Exam focus

In your exam you should set up the relevant statement of financial position or statement of profit or loss proforma first and then slot in the numbers from the TB. Make any required adjustments to the numbers from the TB in bracketed workings on the face of your proforma statement. Remember to deal with the easiest adjustments first.

Common year-end adjustments

1 Opening and closing inventory

Opening inventory (per TB) is $7,650. Closing inventory is $8,490.

Opening inventory (P&L)

2 From SOFP	7,650		

Inventory (SFP)

1 per TB	7,650	2 Trading account balance	7,650
3 Closing inventory	8,490	Bal c/f	8,490
	16,140		16,140
Bal b/f	8,490		

Closing inventory (P&L)

	8,490	3 Closing inventory	8,490

1 Opening balance of $7,650 is b/d on the statement of financial position inventory account.

2 The opening balance is transferred out of the statement of financial position to the opening inventory account in the statement of profit or loss.

	Dr	**Cr**
Dr Opening inventory (P&L)	7,650	
Cr Inventory (SFP)		7,650

3 Closing inventory is recorded in both the statement of financial position and statement of profit or loss.

Dr Inventory (SFP)	8,490	
Cr Closing inventory (P&L)		8,490

2 Non-current asset disposals

Van disposed of. Trade in value (part exchange value) $1,000 and cost of new van $3,200. Cost of old van, $2,100; accumulated depreciation $1,000.

Van (cost) account

Old van	2,100	1 Disposals	2,100
3 New van – cash	2,200	Balance c/f	3,200
3 P/E value	1,000		
	5,300		**5,300**
Balance b/f	3,200		

Old van disposal account

1 Van cost	2,100	2 Accum dept	1,000
		3 P/E value	1,000
		4 Loss	100
	2,100		**2,100**

Old van accumulated depreciation

2 Disposals	1,000	2 Depreciation b/f	1,000

		Dr	Cr
1	Transfer cost of original van to disposal account		
	Dr Disposals with old van cost	2,100	
	Cr Van account with old van cost		2,100
2	Transfer accumulated depreciation on original van to disposal account		
	Dr Accumulated depreciation with depreciation to date	1,000	
	Cr Disposals with depreciation to date		1,000
3	Account for disposal proceeds of old van/Purchase of new van		
	Dr Van account with total value ($2,200 cash + $1,000 p/e)	3,200	
	Cr Cash with cash paid (account not shown)		2,200
	Cr Disposals with part exchange amount		1,000
4	Calculate profit/loss on sale		
	Dr Statement of profit or loss with loss	100	
	Cr Disposals with loss (balancing figure on account)		100

3 Allowance for receivables

An allowance for receivables of $538 is required at the end of the year.
Total receivables = $10,760. Opening allowances $437.

Allowance for receivables

1 Bal c/f	538	Per TB	437
		Irrecoverable debts	101
	538		**538**
		Balance b/f	538

Irrecoverable debts expense

Per TB	1,791	Profit or loss	1,892
Allow for receivables	101		
	1,892		**1,892**

		Dr	Cr
1	**Account for increase in allowance**		
	Dr Irrecoverable debts expense	101	
	Cr Allowance for receivables with balancing figure on this a/c		101
2	**Close irrecoverable debts expense to statement of profit or loss**		
	Dr Statement of profit or loss	1,892	
	Cr Irrecoverable debts expense with total charge for year		1,892

3 Other adjustments

Irrecoverable debts

Dr Irrecoverable debts expense	X
Cr RLCA	X

Depreciation expense

Dr Depreciation expense	X
Cr Accumulated depreciation	X

Accruals

Dr Expense account	X
Cr Accruals (SFP)	X

Prepayments

Dr Prepayments (SFP)	X
Cr Expense account	X

Closing the books

After the final accounts have been prepared, the books are closed:

1. Transfer the balances on all statement of profit or loss accounts to the statement of profit or loss ledger.
2. Transfer the final balance on the statement of profit or loss account (the profit or loss) to the capital account.
3. Transfer the balance on the drawings account to the capital account.

Capital account

		B/f	8,000
3 Drawings	3,750	2 Profit	2,000
C/f	6,250		
	10,000		10,000
		B/f	6,250

This process ensures that income and expense accounts and the drawings account are 'cleared out' and start from a nil position in the new accounting period.

chapter

13

Partnership accounts

In this chapter

- Partnership agreements.
- Advantages and disadvantages of partnerships.
- Partnership accounts – overview.
- Partnership accounts.
- Profit appropriation.
- Other key points.
- Guaranteed minimum profit shares.
- Partnership financial statements.

Partnership agreements

Definition

A partnership is two or more individuals working together, normally with some agreement drawn up between them.

Partnership Agreement
= agreement, not necessarily written, which governs relationships between partners. Matters normally included: • Name of firm, type of business, duration • Amounts of capital introduced • Distribution of profits • Drawings allowed • Arrangements for dissolution • Setting of disputes • Preparation and audit of accounts.

Advantages and disadvantages of partnerships

Advantages of partnership	Disadvantages of partnership
• Business risk spread between partners. • Individual partners develop specific skills for partnership – not 'jack of all trades'. • Provides more capital for business. • Continuation of the business if one partner dies or retires.	• Disputes between partners e.g. on direction of business. • Joint and several liability – all partners liable for business debts, no matter which partner incurred them. • Discussion amongst partners may mean it takes longer to make business decisions.

Partnership accounts – overview

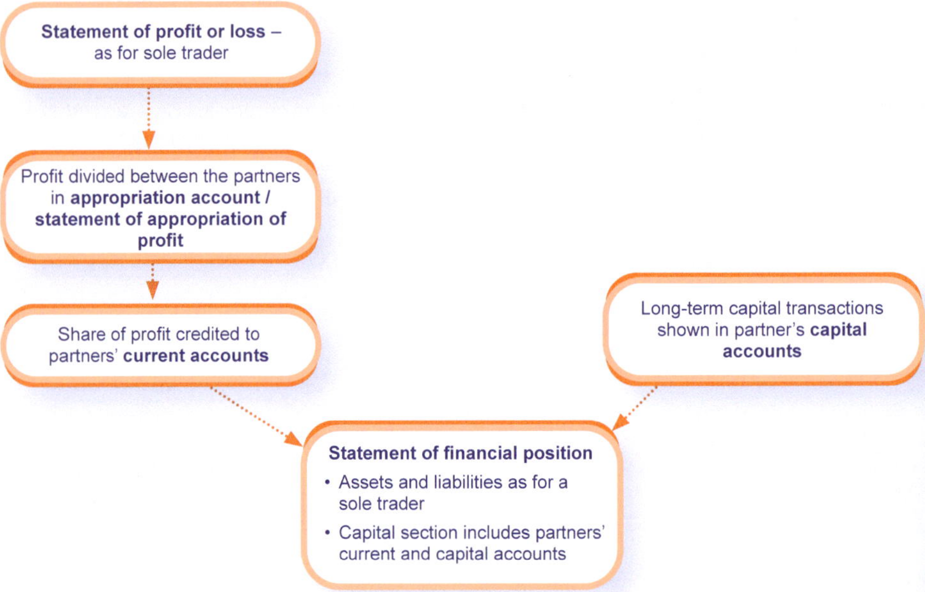

Partnership accounts

Capital accounts

- Show capital introduced into partnership.
- Only change when capital is amended (introduced or withdrawn, normally on change in partnership).
- Partners may receive notional interest on amount of capital invested in partnership.

Partners' Capital accounts

	Ant	Bee		Ant	Bee
			Balance b/f	5,000	10,000
Balance c/f	5,000	10,000			
	5,000	10,000		5,000	10,000

Current accounts

- Show current amount owing/ owed between partnership and each partner.
- Receive profit share for year and show drawings made by each partner.

Partners' current accounts

	Ant	Bee		Ant	Bee
Drawings	2,500	11,000	Balance b/f	3,750	8,000
Balance c/f	6,250	2,000	Profit	5,000	5,000
	8,750	**13,000**		**8,750**	**13,000**

Profit appropriation account

- Shows split of profit for year between partners.
- Profit split depends on partnership agreement.

Appropriation account

Share of profit		Net Profit	
Ant	5,000		
Bee	5,000		
	10,000		10,000

Statement of financial position presentation

- Partners' accounts shown separately on statement of financial position.

Partners' accounts	Capital	Current	Total
Ant	5,000	6,250	11,250
Bee	10,000	2,000	12,000
	15,000	**8,250**	**23,250**

Profit appropriation

May be up to four elements:

1 Interest on capital
2 Salaries
3 Interest on drawings
4 Profit share

Always calculate the profit share last.

Partners' accounts	Ant	Bee	Total
Interest on capital @ 8%	400	800	1,200
Salaries (assumed)	2,000	3,000	5,000
Interest on drawings @ 2%	(50)	(220)	(270)
Profit share 2:3	1,628	2,442	4,070
	3,978	6,022	10,000

Note: this example assumes drawings were made at the start of the year and so a full year's interest is charged.

Double entry:

Appropriation of profit: Ant and Bee partnership	Dr	Cr
1 Dr Statement of profit or loss	10,000	
Cr Appropriation account		10,000
2 Dr Appropriation account	10,000	
Cr Ant current account		3,978
Cr Bee current account		6,022

Other key points

Drawings	Partner makes loan to partnership	Partners' salaries
• May attract interest during the year. • Effectively means increase in profits for appropriation. • Interest is calculated from the date of withdrawal.	• Amount over and above capital. • Normally temporary. • Treat as if loan made by third party. • Interest therefore charged to statement of profit or loss.	• Are appropriation of profit (not an expense like employees' salaries). • Salaries are not necessarily withdrawn by partners.

Guaranteed minimum profit shares

- Some partnerships guarantee minimum profit share to some partners.
- Where profit insufficient to pay this, other partners make good in proportion to their profit-sharing ratio.

Example

- A, B and C share profits 1:2:3
- A has a guaranteed profit of $5,000
- If A's profit is only $2,500, then B and C make up $2,500 in ratio 2:3
- B pays $1,000 and C pays $1,500

Partnership financial statements

Prepare as follows:

Statement of profit or loss	Statement of financial position
• Prepare as for sole trader to net profit. • Calculate split of net profit per appropriation rules. • Transfer profit shares to partners' current accounts. • Deduct drawings from current accounts.	• Prepare as for sole trader for assets and liabilities. • Capital account of sole trader replaced with balances on partners' capital and current accounts.

Exam focus

The most complicated section of partnerships is the appropriation of profit. Remember that interest on capital, partner's salaries, interest on drawings and finally the profit share all form part of this calculation.

An exam question will not ask for full partnership accounts, but is likely to require a working showing the division of profit and possibly capital and current accounts.

chapter

14

Incomplete records

In this chapter

- Net asset approach.
- Using cost structures to find missing figures.
- Using ledger accounts to find missing figures.
- Incomplete records – question approach.

Net asset approach

Find profit based on change in net assets over the year.

1 Prepare assets and liabilities of statement of financial position at the end of the year – that is to find net assets.

2 Prepare similar statement of financial position at the end of last year (normally given in the question).

3 Calculate difference between the two net assets figures.

4 Deduct capital introduced.

5 Add drawings.

6 This gives the profit for the year.

Statement of financial position	This year	Last year
Non-current assets	14,000	10,000
Receivables	12,100	6,000
Inventory	23,000	18,500
Cash and bank	15,000	14,500
Payables	(8,000)	(7,500)
Net assets	56,100	41,500
Increase in net assets		14,600
Less capital introduced in year		(5,000)
Add drawings for year		15,000
Profit for the year		24,600

You may be required to make adjustments to this year's statement of financial position figures:

Typical exam comment	Working
CA of non-current assets b/f was 15,000. New machine purchased for 6,000 and old machine with CA of 3,000 disposed of. Depreciation charge was 4,000.	**Non-current assets** CV b/f + Purchases in year – Disposals (at CV) – Depreciation for year = CA c/f **15,000** **6,000** **3,000** **4,000** **14,000**
The balance on the receivables ledger control account (some questions state the list of unpaid invoices) was 12,300 which includes 200 of debts against which an allowance is required.	**Receivables** Amount per RLCA – Allowance for receiva-bles = Net receivables on statement of financial position **12,300** **200** **12,100**
The value of inventory from the year-end inventory count and valuation was 25,000 although a provision of 2,000 is required against some obsolete inventory.	**Inventory** Cost – Adjustment to NRV = Statement of financial position value **25,000** **2,000** **23,000**

Exam focus

Remember profit is being determined by finding the difference between two statement of financial position. The information provided may look complicated, but follow the procedure outlined above and you will be able to find the profit figure.

Using cost structures to find missing figures

Cost structures

Definition

Gross profit percentage

= profit made per $100 of sales expressed as a percentage

Mark up

= amount of profit added to cost to obtain the selling price. Often expressed as a percentage of cost

Examples

Jones applies a mark up of 40% to purchases. Sales for the year are $150,000. What is gross profit?

Exam focus

The examiner frequently comments that students confuse mark up and margin. You must be able to distinguish these terms.

	Gross profit percentage		Mark up	
Sales	10,000	100%	12,000	120%
Cost of sales	8,000	80%	10,000	100%
Gross profit	**2,000**	**20%**	**2,000**	**20%**

Gross profit percentage **Gross profit**

Sales	10,000	100%
Cost of sales	8,000	80%
Gross profit	**2,000**	**20%**

$$150{,}000 \times \frac{40\%}{140\%} = 42{,}857$$

Filbert achieves a 25% gross margin. What level of sales is needed to obtain $50,000 profit?

	Gross profit	
Sales	?	100%
Cost of sales	?	75%
Gross profit	**50,000**	**25%**

Sales

$$50{,}000 \times \frac{100\%}{25\%} = 200{,}000$$

Using ledger accounts to find missing figures

Cash and bank accounts

Need to complete both accounts to determine missing items e.g. amount of drawings.

Complete cash account first.

1. Enter opening and closing balances

2. Enter cash received from customers

Cash account

Balance b/d	2,000	Banked	38,000
Cash from customers	40,000	Cash expenses	1,000
		Balance c/d	3,000
	42,000		**42,000**

3. Enter any cash payments

4. Amount banked is balancing figure

Then the bank account

1. Enter opening and closing balances

2. Enter amount transferred from cash account as bankings

Bank account

Balance b/d	33,000	Salaries	20,000
From cash account	38,000	Rent	5,000
		Purchases	25,000
		Drawings	? ?
		Balance c/d	5,000
	71,000		**71,000**

3. Enter all cheque payments

4. Find balancing figure

In this case the missing figure of drawings can be determined as $16,000.

Receivables general ledger account

Can be used to find any one missing figure that would normally appear in the account.

Example

Balance b/d on general ledger account was $12,000 and c/d = $16,000. Cash received from customers per bank was $40,000. What was the sales figure?

1 Construct the general ledger account and insert the balances as given.

2 The balancing figure is sales at $44,000.

Receivables general ledger account

Balance b/d	12,000		
Sales	? ?	Cash received	40,000
		Balance c/d	16,000
	56,000		**56,000**

Payables general ledger account

Example

Balance b/d on the account was \$7,000 and c/d = \$5,000. Cash payments to suppliers per bank was \$25,000. What was the purchases figure?

1 Construct the account and insert the balances as given.

2 The balancing figure is purchases at \$23,000.

Payables general ledger account

		Balance b/d	7,000
Payments to suppliers	25,000	Purchases	? ?
Balance c/d	5,000		
	30,000		**30,000**

Trading account and cost structures

Knowledge of the format of the trading account and the cost structure means we can find missing figures in this account.

Procedure outlined below:

1. Set up proforma

2. Enter numbers provided in Q

3. Determine the cost structure

4. Find missing figures

Trading account	$	$	$
Sales	2,000	44,000	200%
Opening inventory	5,000		
Purchases	23,000		
	28,000		
Less closing inventory	? ?		
Cost of sales		? ?	100%
Gross profit		? ?	100%

Cost structure = 100% mark up on goods purchased.

Missing figures

Cost of sales = 50% of sales value (100% mark up) = 22,000

Gross profit = Sales less cost of sales = 22,000

Closing inventory = Cost of sales – Opening inventory – Purchases

= 22,000 – 5,000 – 23,000

= 6,000

Incomplete records – question approach

Summary of question approach below.

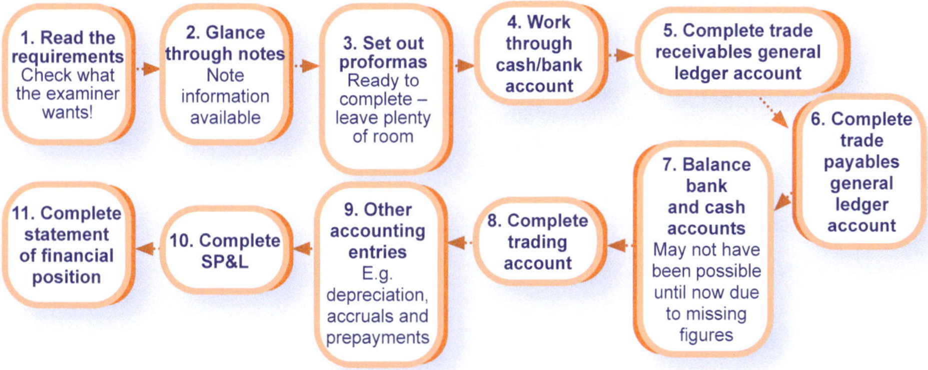

Exam focus

Incomplete records questions appear to contain lots of data. The key to getting good marks is to work through this data methodically following the procedure above. If the statement of financial position doesn't balance then have a quick look at your workings for errors – but if none are obvious then move on. You may lose a mark but this is better than having too little time to complete the other questions in the examination.

References

The Board (2025) *Conceptual Framework For Financial Reporting*. London. IFRS Foundation

The Board (2025) *IAS 2 Inventories.* London. IFRS Foundation

The Board (2025) *IAS 16 Property, Plant and Equipment*. London. IFRS Foundation

The Board (2025) *IAS 37 Provisions, Contingent Liabilities and Contingent Assets.* London. IFRS Foundation

The Board (2025) *IFRS 15 Revenue from Contracts with Customers.* London. IFRS Foundation

The Board (2025) *IFRS 18 Presentation and Disclosure in Financial Statements.* London. IFRS Foundation

Index

A

B

C

D

E

U